AFRICA FOCUS

AFRICAN CULTURE

Rob Bowden and Rosie Wilson

www.heinemannraintree.com
Visit our website to find out more information about Heinemann-Raintree books.

To order:
☎ Phone 888-454-2279
💻 Visit www.heinemannraintree.com to browse our catalog and order online.

©2010 Heinemann Library
an imprint of Capstone Global Library, LLC
Chicago, Illinois

Edited by Louise Galpine and Rachel Howells
Designed by Richard Parker and Manhattan Design
Original illustrations © 2008
Illustrated by Oxford Designers and Illustrators and International Mapping (p.14)
Picture research by Mica Brancic
Originated by Heinemann Library
Printed in China by Leo Paper Products Ltd.

14 13 12 11 10
10 9 8 7 6 5 4 3 2 1

Library of Congress Cataloging-in-Publication Data
Bowden, Rob, 1973-
 African culture / Rob Bowden and Rosie Wilson.
  p. cm. -- (Africa focus)
 Includes bibliographical references and index.
 ISBN 978-1-4329-2440-9 (hc) -- ISBN 978-1-4329-2445-4 (pb)
 1. Africa--Social life and customs. 2. Africa--Civilization. I. Wilson, Rosie. II. Title.
 DT14.B69 2008
 306.096--dc22
                    2008048310

Acknowledgments
We would like to thank the following for permission to reproduce photographs: Alamy p. **40** (© Vehbi Koca); Corbis pp. **8** (© Ed Kashi), **9** (© Nic Bothma/ epa), **11** (© Bob Krist) **15** (© Gideon Mendel), **30** (© Lynn Goldsmith), **34** (© Penny Tweedie); EASI-Images p. **41** (Neil Thomson); Eye Ubiquitous p. **13** (Hutchison); Getty Images pp. **18** (Lonely Planet Images/ Craig Pershouse), **19** (Stuart Price/ Stringer/AFP), **20** (© Per-Anders Pettersson), **25** (Gallo Images/ Martin Harvey), **28** (AFP/ Stringer), **36** (Stone/ Jason Dewey), **39** (© David Levenson); Photolibrary pp. **7** (Oxford Scientific/ © Ariadne Van Zandbergen), **10** (Imagestate/ © Alan Keohane), **16** (Photographer's Choice/ Sylvester Adams), **22** (Paul Nevin), **23** (John Warburton-Lee Photography/ Mark Hannaford), **26** (Japan Travel Bureau/ Haga Library), **29** (Robert Harding Travel/ Peter Groenendijk), **33** (Imagestate/ David South).

Cover photograph of women performing a traditional dance in Ethiopia's Ogaden region, reproduced with permission of Reuters (Barry Malone).

We would like to thank Danny Block for his invaluable help in the preparation of this book.

Every effort has been made to contact copyright holders of material reproduced in this book. Any omissions will be rectified in subsequent printings if notice is given to the publishers.

All the Internet addresses (URLs) given in this book were valid at the time of going to press. However, due to the dynamic nature of the Internet, some addresses may have changed, or sites may have changed or ceased to exist since publication. While the author and Publishers regret any inconvenience this may cause readers, no responsibility for any such changes can be accepted by either the author or the Publishers.

Contents

Some words are printed in bold, **like this**. You can find out what they mean by looking in the glossary on page 44.

Introduction to Africa

Africa is the world's second-largest **continent** and has 53 individual countries. The continent is so large that you could fit the United States, China, and India into it and still have room for all 27 countries of the **European Union (EU)**!

African culture

Africa's landscapes include deserts, forests, mountains, lakes, coasts, and rivers. Its peoples are just as varied. African **culture** grew from the ways in which Africa's people relate to their environment and to one another. It is about how people live and what they do and enjoy. African traditions, behavior, language, dress, food, music, and art are all parts of African culture. With so many different peoples and landscapes, African culture is extremely varied.

Cultural changes

African cultures have spread their influence to other parts of the world for a long time. This happened especially between the 1300s and 1800s, when thousands of African **slaves** were sent to the Americas and took their cultures with them. Earlier, **trade** and **immigration** also brought African culture to different regions.

African cultures have also been influenced by people from outside Africa for thousands of years. **Islam**, for example, came to North Africa with traders from the Middle East. During the 1800s and 1900s, European **colonization** of Africa had a major impact on African culture. European languages were introduced and new land boundaries divided traditional cultural groups.

21st-century Africa

Today Africa continues to change. Improved transportation systems and technology such as television and the Internet allow African cultures to mix with other cultures more easily. This is creating exciting new chapters in the story of Africa's long and fascinating culture.

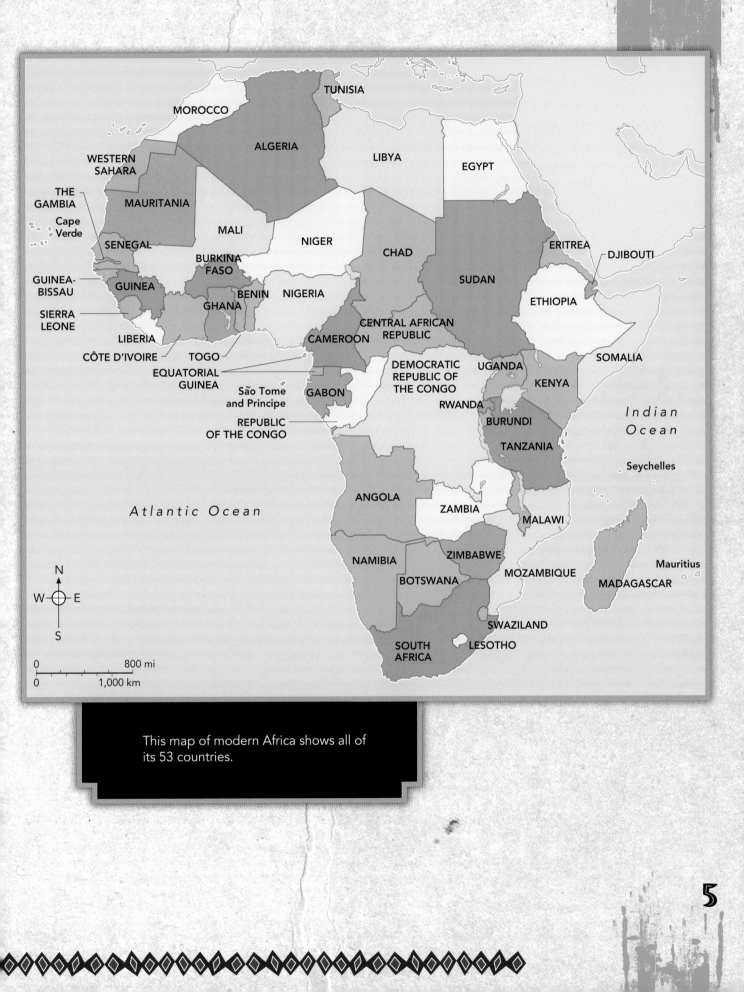

This map of modern Africa shows all of its 53 countries.

African Traditions

The first humans are thought to have come from Africa and then spread slowly around the world. In much of the world, the ancient traditions of these early humans are long lost. But they can still be found in some parts of Africa, despite thousands of years of change. The Kalahari San people of Botswana and Namibia, for example, lead a hunting and gathering lifestyle that **archeologists** believe is similar to that of the first humans.

AFRICA FACT
Human bones dating back around 1.2 million years show that the first humans probably came from Africa. The bones were discovered at Olduvai Gorge in Tanzania and Lake Turkana in Kenya.

Kalahari San

Ancient rock paintings in southern Africa show us that the San people have lived in the Kalahari Desert for at least 10,000 years. Many of their ways of living have changed little, such as being able to move easily by staying in small family groups and having few possessions. Their lack of possessions means the San are very creative. They use their hunting bows as musical instruments, for example. Sounds are made by playing the bow string with the mouth or against a hollow container.

Ancient societies

Some of the world's oldest known societies (groups of people) are African. The remains of artwork and jewelry found in southern Africa are signs that there were organized societies there up to 100,000 years ago. Rock paintings found in the Sahara Desert show that people had begun to farm **crops** and animals by around 9000 BCE. These early forms of farming were the secret to the success of Africa's most famous early society, the ancient Egyptians. They lived in the Nile Valley of Egypt in around 3100–1200 BCE.

The San of the Kalahari Desert in southern Africa hunt with a bow and arrow. Their lifestyle and culture are thought to be similar to that of the earliest humans.

Villagers in the Niger Delta celebrate a local harvest festival called *Funfu Ma Tie*, which dates back to the 16th century.

Harvest festivals

Farming has always been important to the people of Africa. Many festivals and **customs** are about celebrating a good **harvest**. Yams (a potatolike crop) are the main food of the Igbo people of Nigeria. Each year in August they celebrate the yam harvest with a festival called *Iwa-ji*, meaning "new yam." **Rituals** are performed to thank God and the **ancestors** for a good harvest. The community gathers to celebrate with music and dancing and to taste the yams!

Naming ceremonies

Names are important in Africa. They can tell others where you are from, what was happening when you were born, whether you are a twin, or even on what day you were born. In Ghana, the Akan people give their children one name based on the day of the week they were born. Each week day has different male or female names. The main names are shown in the table below.

Day of the week	Male name	Female name
Sunday	Kwesi, Kwasi, Akwesi	Akosua, Akousia, Esi
Monday	Kwodwo, Kwadwo, Kojo	Adwoa, Adjoa
Tuesday	Kobena , Kwabena	Abenaa
Wednesday	Kweku, Kwaku, Ako	Ekua, Akua, Aquia, Akwia
Thursday	Yaw, Yao, Yawu, Kwaw, Kwao	Yaa, Aba
Friday	Kofi, Kwafi	Efua, Afua, Afia
Saturday	Kwame, Kwamena	Ama, Amma, Amba, Ame

Africa Fact

Akan birthday names are also called "soul names" and describe what type of person you are supposed to be. According to tradition, you are calm and peaceful if born on a Monday and a wanderer or traveler if born on a Friday.

Old and new

Modern life in Africa is very different from the past, but traditions are still strong. When people become ill they may visit a local healer instead of a modern doctor, for example. People starting a new business may still make **offerings** to the ancestors in the belief that will bring them good luck. Tradition has also survived in clothing styles. Even modern clothing often uses traditional patterns, shapes, and colors.

A model wears an outfit by the designer Akinka from Burundi during Cape Town Fashion Week. Modern African fashion is often an exciting mix of the old and new.

Peoples and Languages

African people

A group of people who share the same background are known as an **ethnic group**. They normally have similar physical characteristics, share the same **customs**, and speak the same language. Africa has hundreds of ethnic groups and at least 1,500 spoken languages.

In the past, ethnic groups in Africa were often limited to specific areas, but over hundreds of years people have moved around, and ethnic groups have become mixed up. In parts of Uganda, for example, it is possible to find more than 15 different ethnic groups living in a single village.

North African Berbers

The Berbers mainly live in the deserts and mountains of North Africa, where they farm **livestock**. They live in groups called **clans**, which are made up of several related families. The clans also group together to form communities with an elected leader or chieftain.

Some Berber communities are **nomadic**. This means they move from place to place to find food and water for themselves and their livestock. Other Berbers have land on the edge of the desert, where they grow **crops** during the winter. In the hot summers they leave their fields and live in the cooler mountains with their livestock.

Berber herdsmen trade sheep and goats at a market in Imilchil, Morocco.

Dogon tribesmen wear traditional costumes and masks during a festival in Bamako, Mali.

The Dogon of Mali

The Dogon people live in the mountains and central **plateau** of Mali, in West Africa. Most of them are farmers, but some are highly skilled at making crafts. The Dogon have a spiritual leader called a "hogon" who is an important symbol of Dogon beliefs. These beliefs are based on their knowledge of the stars.

Masai Warriors

The Masai people live in Kenya and Tanzania. They are traditionally nomadic people who survive on the meat, blood, and milk of cattle. They live in clans that are ruled by men and organized by age. When a boy reaches 14 years, he takes part in a ceremony to become a *moran*, or **warrior**. He then spends up to 15 years living away from his family in the African **bush** with other morans. He trains to be strong and fearless and learns tribal customs. Later, he will become a senior warrior, junior elder, and then senior elder. Only senior elders can make decisions for the whole clan.

Rise of the Zulu

The Zulu people live in highly organized societies in South Africa. Families live in clans that are ruled by the oldest Zulu man in the clan. The Zulu are famous warriors. They were once led by the fearsome Shaka (around 1787–1828). Shaka led his armies to attack neighboring clans and tribes, which made the Zulu into the largest ethnic group in South Africa. It is said that more than two million people were killed by Shaka and his warriors. The Zulu now live peacefully with other people in South Africa, but still have great pride in their past. They have kept traditions such as their strictly organized society.

Madagascar

Madagascar is a large island off the southeast coast of Africa. The Madagascan people have close cultural links with Southeast Asia and do not consider themselves to be African. Their language, called Malagasy, is related to languages from Indonesia (these languages are known as Austronesian—see the map on page 14). The island and its people have been treated as part of Africa since they were **colonized** by France between 1896 and 1958. French is still a national language in Madagascar today.

These men are morans (young warriors) of the Masai tribe. They are preparing for a ceremony that boys go through to become men.

Languages

Africa has more than 1,500 languages, with more than 300 spoken in Nigeria alone! When languages are different but share some features, they are part of a **language family**. In addition to the Austronesian languages, Africa has four main language families.

- In North Africa people speak Afro-Asiatic languages. These include Arabic, Berber, and Hausa.

- South of the Sahara Desert most Africans speak Niger-Congo languages. There are around 1,400 of these languages, including Zulu, Mande, and Kikuyu.

- Where the northern and southern language families meet, there is a group of languages called the Nilo-Saharan languages. The Masai and Turkana are examples of people who speak these languages.

- The last language family is the Khoisan languages of southern Africa, which are known for their use of "clicks." They are spoken by people such as the San of the Kalahari Desert.

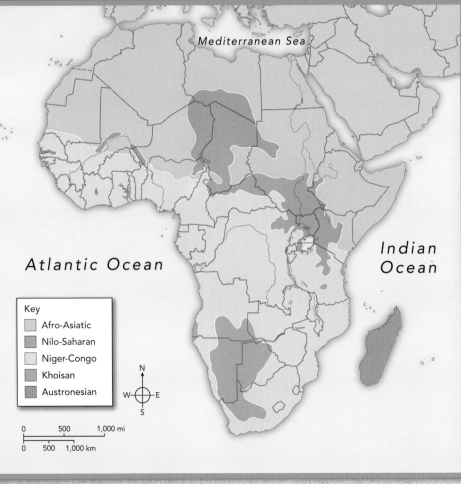

Key
- Afro-Asiatic
- Nilo-Saharan
- Niger-Congo
- Khoisan
- Austronesian

Mediterranean Sea

Atlantic Ocean

Indian Ocean

N
W E
S

0   500   1,000 mi
0   500   1,000 km

This map shows the main language families of Africa. Experts are still figuring out exactly how many languages there are within these bigger groups.

A woman stands in front of human skulls at Ntamara Church in Kigali, Rwanda. Around one million people were killed when Hutu and Tutsi tribal groups began to fight for control of Rwanda in 1994. The two tribes are very similar. They speak the same language, live in the same areas, and follow the same traditions. However, Belgian colonists thought the Tutsis were superior to the Hutus, and this is how the trouble began.

Common voices

To help communication between Africa's many different people, Africa has adopted several common languages. These are some people's first language, but are more often used as a second language that allows people to communicate more easily.

- The most commonly spoken language in Africa is Arabic. It is especially important in North Africa and helps the region to have strong **trade** and cultural links with Arabic-speaking countries in the Middle East.

- English is the most widespread language in Africa. It arrived with English-speaking **missionaries** and spread during the **colonial** period. French was also introduced as a common colonial language and is still widely used in West Africa.

- Swahili is a common African language that began on Zanzibar and the East African coast. Today it is a trade and cultural language used in East Africa. Fulani is another common African language and is widely used in West Africa.

Family and Daily Life

Daily life in Africa is extremely varied. People living in **rural** areas may have very different lives from those living in Africa's cities. Despite such differences, some parts of daily life are similar across the **continent**. Men are usually the head of communities and families, for example. The family unit is of great importance to African life and can be very large.

Changing family life

In the past, many African families lived close to one another in the same village or area, but this way of life is now less common. One reason for this is that more people are leaving rural areas to live in towns and cities. This is called **urbanization**. It is harder for families to live together in **urban** housing, which is normally more crowded and expensive than in rural areas. Almost 40 percent of all Africans were living in a town or city in 2007, and the number was increasing by around 1,500 people every hour!

Traditional clothing, such as these loose flowing cotton robes, are well suited to the climate in Cameroon. They remain popular even when Western-style clothes are easily available.

Elders

Older people are treated with great respect in African **culture** and are commonly known as elders. They are often selected as political and social leaders because of their greater knowledge of life. Some people become elders based on power and wealth, and some are elected to be elders after people vote for them. In societies such as the Zulu or Masai, a man becomes an elder automatically once he reaches a certain age.

Elders play an important part in preserving African societies. Traditionally, elders were responsible for using spoken words to pass down the knowledge, history, and culture of their people. It is only quite recently that these things have been written down instead.

AFRICA FACT

Africa's population is younger than anywhere else in the world. In Central and East Africa, around half the population is under 18 years of age.

Women in Africa

Most African societies are led by men, but women often have the most important roles in daily life. Women will often lead children in helping with tasks such as farming, cooking, shopping, and caring for children. They also cook the family meal and may earn an **income** by selling things or having a job. As more Africans move to cities and leave traditional societies behind, women are giving birth to fewer children.

These women are discussing the price of bowls and plates in Togo. Markets such as this can be found around Africa and act as an important social center.

AFRICA FACT

In some African societies, men have more than one wife. This is called polygamy. In polygamous families the first wife is normally in charge of the other wives.

African food

Food is important in African life, and each region has its own specialities. Some of these are known outside Africa, too, such as tagine (stew) from Morocco and biltong (dried meat) from South Africa. Lesser-known specialities include matoke from Uganda, which is a type of plantain (a fruit similar to banana) eaten with a rich groundnut (peanut) sauce. Food is often based on what is locally available, so seafood, such as octopus, is popular in stews in the Cape Verde islands.

Hunger and diet

Not everyone in Africa has enough food to eat, and many people go hungry. Another problem for Africa is that even when people do have food, their diet can be very poor. They may eat only the same foods, such as corn or millet (a type of grain), every day. Eating only a few foods means that people are missing important **nutrients**, which the body needs to stay fit and healthy.

Education

Fewer African children attend school than in most of the rest of the world. This is considered a major problem for the people of Africa, but just as important is the type of education people have. In many countries the education system was introduced by **colonial** powers and ignores local knowledge and values. Many educated Africans find that their qualifications do not fit the system in Africa.

Students sit in a crowded schoolroom in Kampala, Uganda. Like many African schools, it has only basic facilities.

Basic needs

Because of poverty, not everyone in Africa has food, water, **hygiene**, and housing. People who lack these things are more at risk of disease and illness. Education can play an important part in reducing risks by teaching people how to prepare food safely and how to make water safe for drinking. Art and drama are sometimes used to teach health messages to people who cannot read or write.

Young girls take water away from a pump in Galufu, Malawi. Safe water sources such as this dramatically improve the health of Africa's poorest people.

Killer diseases

Malaria is a disease that is spread by the bite of a mosquito. It is one of the biggest causes of death in Africa. About one million people die from malaria in Africa every year, and most of these deaths are among children under five years.

Another killer disease is **HIV/AIDS**. Africa has more people with HIV/AIDS than anywhere else in the world. Southern Africa has been hit hard by the disease, and many adults have died from it. The **economy** has suffered because many of those who have become ill or have died are workers. Some families are now made up of grandparents and children only—South Africa alone has more than 1.4 million AIDS **orphans**.

Biography — Nkosi Johnson

Nkosi Johnson was born with the disease HIV/AIDS in 1989. As a boy he campaigned for better medical care and treatment for people living with HIV/AIDS. In July 2000, a year before he died, he made a famous speech at an international conference on the disease. He said:

"Care for us and accept us—we are all human beings. We are normal. We have hands. We have feet. We can walk, we can talk, we have needs just like everyone else—don't be afraid of us—we are all the same!"

The music of work

Many types of African singing come from work songs that help motivate workers. The songs, for example, often have a rhythm for digging the soil or pulling in fishing nets. **Jazz**, **blues**, and **gospel** music were all influenced by African work songs that were brought to the Americas by African **slaves**.

Men work together to thresh grain in Ethiopia. Across Africa, activities are often performed in groups. Songs are also sung to keep a rhythm and motivate one another.

Children at play

In many African households, children are expected to help with chores such as cooking, cleaning, and caring for children, but they still find time to play! Singing games and team games are popular and do not involve any special equipment. Toys in shops are too expensive for many children to afford, so children across Africa have become experts at making their own toys. They use local materials, including other people's garbage, to make go-carts, pinwheels, or balls. In Malawi, children make brightly colored cars, bicycles, and trucks called *Galimoto* from old wire and waste metal. Some of these toys are considered art by tourists to Africa, who often buy them to take home as souvenirs.

Sport and leisure

Long-distance running is a global sport that is dominated by African runners. Men and women from Kenya and Ethiopia have been especially successful and hold most of the World and Olympic records (see the table below).

A boy in the Maluti mountains of Lesotho plays with a toy guitar made from local waste materials. Many African children have become skilled at turning waste products into toys.

Long distance runner	World records held
Haile Gebrselassie (Ethiopia; male runner)	10 km (6 miles) 20 km (12 miles) 20,000 meters (12 miles) Marathon One hour run
Tegla Loroupe (Kenya; female runner)	20,000 meters (12 miles) 25,000 meters (16 miles) 30,000 meters (19 miles)

Football is more popular and widespread in Africa than running. Some of the world's best soccer players are African, but they play mostly in European soccer clubs where they can earn more money. The Africa Cup of Nations is the region's most important soccer tournament and takes place every two years. Egypt won the tournament in 2008. The soccer World Cup final will be held in South Africa in 2010.

Religion, Beliefs, and Customs

The beliefs and **customs** of different African **cultures** go back hundreds or even thousands of years, but day-to-day beliefs in most of Africa today follow major world religions (see the pie chart below). Traditional beliefs have not vanished, however—they are still followed in Angola, the Central African Republic, Madagascar, and Togo. In other countries, traditional beliefs often survive side by side with **mainstream** religions. This mixing of traditional and mainstream beliefs makes religion in Africa very complex.

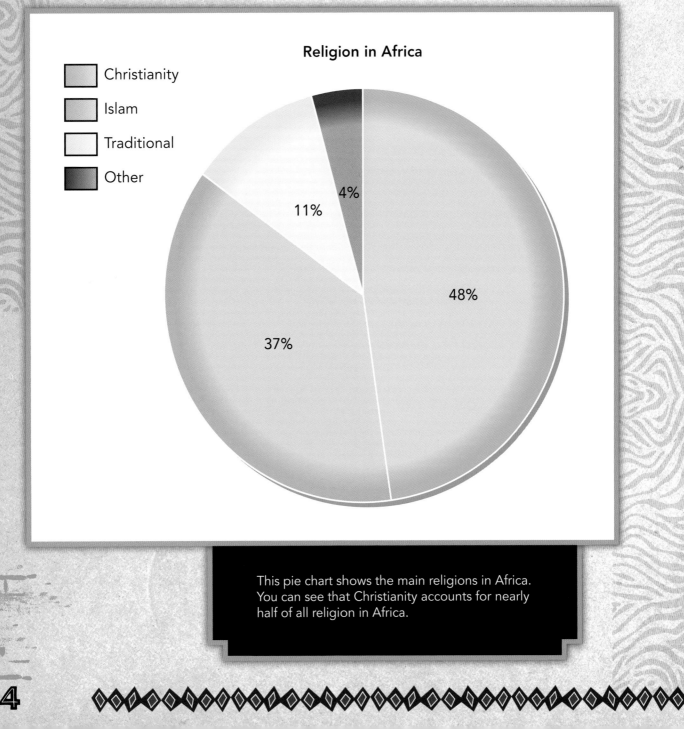

Religion in Africa

- Christianity
- Islam
- Traditional
- Other

4%

11%

48%

37%

This pie chart shows the main religions in Africa. You can see that Christianity accounts for nearly half of all religion in Africa.

Traditional religion

Traditional religions in Africa normally believe in a single "high" god with a number of less powerful deities. These deities are people or things (often on Earth) that are treated as gods. Many religions also have animist beliefs, where an animal, plant, or land feature (such as a mountain) is believed to have a spirit or soul. **Ancestor** worship (the worship of dead relatives) is another important aspect of traditional religions. People visit the **shrines** of their ancestors to make offerings or prayers during celebrations or in times of trouble.

Valuing local beliefs

In modern Africa, traditional beliefs are sometimes thought of as old-fashioned. Traditional medicine, for example, is often rejected for more modern health treatments. This is not true in all places in Africa, however. In Uganda, traditional healers are registered with a national organization called the National Council of Traditional Healers and Herbalists Associations of Uganda (NACOTHA). NACOTHA promotes the positive use of traditional healing in modern Uganda. By registering healers, it hopes to prevent crime by people who pretend to be healers in order to steal money from others.

A woman consults a Sangoma (traditional healer) at Lesedi Cultural Village in South Africa. The village teaches tourists about African culture and helps to keep important traditions alive.

25

The arrival of Christianity

Christianity is the main religion of nearly half the people in Africa. It follows the teachings of Jesus and is thought to have first arrived in Africa (in Egypt) in around 100 CE. This led to the founding of Africa's earliest churches—the Coptic Christian Church in Egypt and the Ethiopian Orthodox Church in Ethiopia. Both churches were established by around 400 CE, and still survive today with around 40 million followers between them. Today, most African Christians live in countries south of the Sahara Desert.

Members of the Ethiopian Orthodox Church celebrate Genna (Christmas) at Lalibela in Ethiopia.

THE ETHIOPIAN CALENDAR

Ethiopia uses a different calendar from the Gregorian calendar used by most of the world. It is based on the calendar of the Ethiopian Orthodox Church and has 13 months instead of 12. It is also seven years and eight months behind the Gregorian calendar. This means that in Ethiopia, they celebrated the first day of the new millennium (January 1, 2000) on what was September 11, 2007 for most of the rest of the world!

Ethiopian month	Gregorian equivalent dates
Meskerem	September 11–October 10 (year starts on September 12 during leap years)
Tikimt	October 11–November 9
Hidar	November 10–December 9
Tahsas	December 10–January 8
Tir	January 9–February 7
Yakatit	February 8–March 9
Magabit	March 10–April 8
Miyazya	April 9–May 8
Ginbot	May 9–June 7
Sene	June 8–July 7
Hamle	July 8–August 6
Nehasa	August 7–September 5
Pagumiene	September 6–10 (year ends on September 11 during leap years)

Christian missions

Christianity spread across most of Africa following the arrival of Christians from Europe. They first came as explorers and traders and later as **missionaries** and **colonial** settlers. Christian missionaries came to Africa to spread Christianity and do what they believed was the work of God. They built schools and hospitals to provide for local people as well as building churches for worship. European and American Christian organizations are still active in Africa today and continue to run many schools and hospitals.

African Christianity

African Christianity has developed its own style by mixing local culture with mainstream beliefs. Christian churches in Africa often make use of the continent's long tradition of song and dance. African churches can be quite strict, too. Their leaders do not always agree with the more relaxed rules being introduced by some Christian Churches in Europe and America. Many disagree with giving women more power in the Church, for example.

Islam

Islam is Africa's second-largest religion, and just over one-third of Africans are Muslim. Islam is the main religion of North Africa and also has large numbers of followers in West and East Africa.

Muslims believe in one God, Allah. They also worship the Prophet Muhammad, who lived from 570 to 632 CE. His teachings, written in the **Koran**, mention five pillars of Islam that all Muslims must perform during their lifetime. One of these is the "hajj." This is a pilgrimage (spiritual journey) to Mecca in Saudi Arabia, the holiest place in Islam. For many Africans, this is an expensive and difficult journey. Poor transportation systems mean that many who would like to make the pilgrimage are unable to complete their journey.

The spread of Islam

Islam arrived in Africa with traders from the Middle East. They traveled across the Sahara Desert into North Africa, and across the Arabian Sea to East Africa. Many of these traders brought new knowledge with them from Islamic scholars. Islamic schools were set up to share this knowledge as well as the beliefs of Islam. Muslim schools, or madrassahs, where children learn the teachings of Islam, are still popular today.

Students learn how to write verses of the Koran at an Islamic school near Khartoum, Sudan.

A man of the Sufi branch of Islam dances himself into a trance in Omdurman, Sudan. Those performing this dance are known as "whirling dervishes."

Islamic culture

Islam has a varied influence on the customs and lifestyles of Africans. Northern Nigeria, for example, has introduced strict Islamic law (Sharia), with severe punishments for those who fail to follow it. In South Africa, by comparison, Muslims enjoy much greater freedoms and mix their religion with other cultural influences.

In many parts of Africa, Muslim men and women wear traditional Islamic clothing. This is based on cool, full-length robes that cover much of the body. Women are often required to cover their heads with a *hijab* (headscarf) and their faces with a *niqab* (veil).

Performing Arts

Africans use art in the way they dress, communicate, and share stories. Even household tools such as cooking pots are skillfully created to be beautiful as well as useful. Some forms of art are shared across many African countries, such as a general skill in pottery or a love of dancing. Other art is even more local and represents the **culture** of particular **ethnic groups**.

Miriam Makeba, or "Mama Afrika," was one of Africa's most famous singers and performed all over the world until her death in 2008.

African voices

Africans use their voices in a wide variety of singing styles, and have a huge range of different notes and sounds. African voices are also used in storytelling, sometimes with music, to teach people about **morals** and history. Some of these stories have turned into common sayings or **proverbs**. Others have become songs that are now rehearsed and performed for pleasure as much as for their message.

Theater

Drama and theater in Africa started with people acting out traditional stories. Today, modern drama follows a similar pattern and is helping to keep many African traditions alive.

The power of drama to tell stories and communicate with people is also being used to help with some of Africa's problems. Theater groups, for example, have developed plays about the risk of **HIV/AIDS**. They raise awareness of the disease by performing in schools and communities.

Dance

Dance in Africa is performed during celebrations and **rituals**. Dance is part of healing rituals and religious and spiritual **customs**, such as those of the Sufi Muslims in Sudan and Egypt. The Sufi use a spinning dance to create a **trance** that they believe brings them closer to God (also see page 29).

Another style of dance is the jumping dance performed by Masai men in East Africa. This dance is used to show their strength as **warriors**—the higher they jump, the stronger they are thought to be!

African music

Music plays an important role in African culture, but African music has also become famous and popular outside Africa. In Africa, celebrations and rituals almost always include music, and music is popular in the workplace—especially when a team of people are working together. Many traditional songs are types of farming song, such as the songs of Turkana men in northern Kenya that come from singing to their cattle.

Modern African music uses many traditional rhythms, instruments, and sounds, but often adds non-African influences to create new styles of music. This is sometimes known as fusion music because it is fusing different styles together.

Urban artists

Positive Black Soul is a hip-hop group based in Dakar, Senegal. They rap in English, French, and Wolof, a Senegalese language. They went on a 13-country tour called the "African Presidents Tour" in 2005 and have also performed and recorded in Paris and New York. One of the members of the group is DJ Awadi, who works with UN-HABITAT to help educate young people. He also speaks about important issues in Africa.

African instruments

Africa has a range of musical instruments, but its skills in drum making are famous. A drum is normally carved from wood with an animal skin (or sometimes a fish skin) stretched across it. They come in many different styles. The drum is played with either hands or sticks to create the rhythm for much African music.

Another common African instrument is the thumb piano. It has metal or bamboo keys of different sizes , which are twanged with the thumb to produce notes.

Drumming is popular in many African countries. These drummers are members of the Dogon ethnic group in Mali in West Africa.

AFRICA FACT

Because the sound of a drum carries farther than a human voice, drums have long been used to send messages in Africa. They are particularly used by forest communities, such as the pygmies of Central Africa.

Visual Arts

African crafts use mainly local materials and so vary greatly across the **continent**. Among the most important materials are wood, stone, metals, and plants (especially grasses and seeds).

The weaving of natural grasses to make baskets is a craft found in many parts of Africa. These baskets are often simple and meet practical needs. In countries such as Uganda and Rwanda, the grasses are dyed in bright colors and used to create beautiful patterns.

Batik

Batik is one of the most common types of **textile** art in Africa. It uses a combination of dyes to create designs for clothing or pictures. A rice paste or wax is used to prevent parts of the cloth from being dyed. It is later removed to reveal the design. Some of the most complicated batiks can go through this process several times, each time with a different color.

Art from waste

Africans have always been good at using what is around them in an artistic way. This tradition is continuing today with many artists finding interesting uses for waste. Paper is folded and rolled to make beaded jewelry, old tin cans are turned into lanterns, and used plastic bottles are used to make toy cars. Recycled art has become very popular with tourists.

The global crafts market

Some forms of African art have become popular outside Africa. This has created an industry producing African art just for **export**. However, some of the arts and crafts exported are not genuine, and are instead based on what those buying them want to own. Some people fear that this threatens local **culture**, because skills are being used to produce African export art rather than preserve and develop local traditions.

AFRICA FACT

Art pieces made from ivory (elephant tusk) are so valuable that half a million elephants were killed for their tusks in the 1980s. The ivory **trade** was banned in 1989, but an **illegal** trade in ivory continues to threaten the African elephant.

Body decoration

Celebrations and ceremonies often involve body decoration, but in some regions it is a feature of everyday life. In West Africa, decorative scarring is a common form of body art. Patterns are cut into the skin and then left to heal as a scar. In Ethiopia, Mursi and Surma women who are to be married have their lower lip cut in order to fit a lip plate. This is made from clay and inserted in the lower lip, which gradually stretches until it can take a plate that measures up to 8 inches (20 centimeters) across. Women take pride in making and decorating their own lip plates. Some other **ethnic groups** use similar techniques to stretch their earlobes and wear an earplug.

The Wodaabe of the Sahara Desert are one of many ethnic groups who use body art. Wodaabe men use makeup to enhance their faces and make themselves more attractive to women from other Wodaabe clans.

AFRICA FACT

The Fulani people of West Africa hold a male beauty contest called *gerewol*. Young men paint their bodies and decorate them with jewelry before being judged by the young women.

African jewelry

Jewelry is worn by both women and men in Africa. It is normally made using metals and beadwork (using wood, metal, or glass beads). The beadwork of the Samburu in East Africa and the Zulu in South Africa is highly detailed and uses tiny glass beads. Kazuri beads are sold to tourists and exported. Kazuri is a women's organization in Kenya that sells jewelry internationally and uses the money raised to help improve the lives of the women with whom it works.

Painting and modern art

Painting on **canvas** is relatively new to Africa, but some African painters now show their work in galleries around the world. Another common form of painting in Africa is on vehicles and buildings. This type of art is sometimes used for advertising, but can also be just for decoration.

Some artists use modern art to explore Africa's problems. The Nigerian artist Yinka Shonibare explores Africa's **colonial** past and its modern links with Europe. He has done this by creating life-sized models of European colonial scenes using bright African materials and colors.

Africa and Global Culture

As more Africans move to **urban** areas, they come into greater contact with **cultures** from elsewhere in Africa and around the world. This mixing of cultures is helping to create new urban cultures in Africa. It is also creating new audiences for African culture and making it easier for African culture to spread to other parts of the world.

Urban culture

Urban culture in Africa is based around television, music, and film. Music may be local or sometimes it is pop music from Europe or hip hop from the United States. Films and television programs also often come from outside Africa, since few African countries produce their own programs.

South Africa, Egypt, and Nigeria do have television and film industries. Egypt is a major producer of films in Arabic, for example, and sells them throughout the Arab-speaking world. In 2006 the South African film *Tsotsi* won many international awards and created new interest in African filmmaking.

AFRICA FACT

A favorite TV program in Uganda is *Hotsteps Dance*, a reality dance show similar to *Dancing with the Stars*. The show includes international dances such as Calypso, but also local Ugandan styles such as Bakisimba.

Writing Africa

African writing is one of the most influential forms of African culture. Novels and poetry by leading African authors have been read by people around the world.

- Wole Soyinka's plays, books, and poetry are often about the social and political problems of ordinary Nigerians. In 1986 Soyinka was the first black African to receive the Nobel Prize for Literature.

- Chinua Achebe's most famous book is called *Things Fall Apart*. It describes the life of an Igbo community in Nigeria and how it was changed forever by European colonists.

The Nigerian writer Wole Soyinka is pictured above speaking at a book festival. Soyinka is one of Africa's most famous writers and is popular around the world.

New opportunities

New technology such as the Internet, email, and mobile phones is making it easier for African culture to be shared around the world. Mobile phones with cameras, for example, are allowing millions of Africans to take a photograph for the first time! The Internet allows Africans to share ideas with people on the other side of the world. The Internet also allows people to find out more about African culture or to plan a visit to discover Africa for themselves.

African diaspora

Africans who live and work outside Africa and people descended from Africans are known as the African **diaspora**. They are located throughout the world, and many may never have been to Africa. Nevertheless, the African diaspora often feel close ties to Africa or to particular African countries. These ties are often maintained through cultural links such as dress, food, and music. The African diaspora has also played a major role in introducing elements of African culture to places outside Africa. Shops selling African foods, for example, are today common in cities such as London, New York, and Paris.

These Ghanaian women are taking part in a religious ceremony at a church in London, England. They are part of an African diaspora that today lives around the world, but still keeps close contact with Africa and maintains many African customs.

This rooster was made in South Africa from waste plastic. It is an example of modern African art. The chicken was a mascot for the 2007 rugby World Cup that took place in France.

African style

Like all places today, Africa is influenced by many cultures. African culture is not being replaced, however. Instead, people have built on ideas from other cultures to come up with their own "African" alternatives. A good example of this is the popularity of Western-style clothing made with African colors and patterns that have strong links with traditional clothing. The Sakoba Dance Theatre Company from Nigeria mixes traditional Nigerian dances with styles from all over the world in order to promote greater global understanding between cultures.

African style is also influencing design. For example, furniture and **interior design** in Europe now use many ideas that are based on African culture. There are even computer fonts that are based on African traditional culture.

Timeline

3100–1200 Ancient Egypt thrives as one of the world's first great **civilizations** on
BCE the banks of the River Nile in Egypt.

100 CE Christianity arrives in Egypt. By 400 CE the Coptic Church in Egypt and
Ethiopian Orthodox Church in Ethiopia are established.

c.700 **Islam** begins to spread rapidly into North Africa through **trade**
and conquest.

1415 The Portuguese create a trading post at Ceuta in North Africa. This
marks the beginning of European **colonial** interest in Africa.

c.1500 The transatlantic **slave** trade begins to develop, taking slaves from
West Africa to the Americas. Up to 27 million Africans are sold or die as
a result of slavery before it is abolished.

1807–1860 The transatlantic slave trade ends after 400 years of slavery and
around 12 million people being shipped from Africa to the Americas.

1833 Britain passes the Abolition Act to end slavery, and all slaves in the
British Empire are freed. Other nations follow Britain's example.

1865 Slavery ends in the United States.

1884–1885 At the Berlin Conference, European nations who want Africa for its
resources and labor divide up the **continent** into colonies that are
ruled by them.

1948 South Africa's white government introduces a new political system
called **apartheid**, meaning "keep apart". It is designed to keep black
and white South Africans separate.

1950–1970 More than 40 African countries gain independence, but colonialism
still affects people's daily lives.

1957 The first Africa Cup of Nations (soccer tournament) is held in Khartoum,
Sudan, and Egypt wins.

1986   The Nigerian writer Wole Soyinka wins the Nobel Prize for Literature.

1987   The disease **HIV/AIDS** spreads across the continent. The southern African countries, such as South Africa, Botswana, and Swaziland, have high numbers of people living with HIV and dying of AIDS.

1989   A ban on trade in ivory is introduced to protect African elephant numbers.

1994   Apartheid ends in South Africa, and Nelson Mandela is elected president.

1995   Over one-third of Africans now live in urban areas.

2000   Nkosi Johnson, an 11-year-old South African boy, addresses an international conference on HIV/AIDS.

2002   The Soweto Gospel Choir forms in South Africa.

2006   The South African film *Tsotsi* wins an Academy Award for best foreign film.

2010   South Africa becomes the first African country to host the soccer World Cup finals.

Glossary

ancestor family member who has died. Some people pray to their ancestors for good fortune.

apartheid system of separation introduced by the white South African government in 1948. Nonwhite people were sent to separate schools, and even had separate seats in public places.

archeologist person who studies the past by looking at monuments and artifacts from certain cultures

blues style of music developed by African Americans

bush land far away from where people live

canvas cloth used as a background for painting

civilization society with a high level of art, science, and government

clan large group of families who are related to one another

colonial state of being a country that belongs to another country

colonization taking control of another country

continent one of the main areas of land on Earth. Many countries may be found in one continent.

crop plant grown for use by people, such as cereals or vegetables

culture actions and beliefs of a society

custom way of behaving in a certain situation

diaspora movement of people away from their country of origin, or a community made up of people who have left their homeland

economy system under which a country creates, sells, and buys products

ethnic group people who share culture and language

European Union (EU) group of 27 countries in Europe with close political, economic, legal, and social ties

export goods sold to another country; to sell to another country

gospel style of religious music developed by African Americans

harvest season when crops are gathered; to gather a crop

HIV/AIDS the disease AIDS is caused by the HIV virus. HIV attacks the body's ability to protect against infection. There is no cure for HIV or AIDS.

hygiene clean living conditions that prevent disease

illegal against the law

immigration movement of people into a country in order to live there

income money earned through work

interior design decorating a house or room

Islam religion based on the teachings of Prophet Muhammad

jazz style of music developed in the United States

Koran Islam's holy book, where the Prophet Muhammad's teachings are written down

language family languages that share some features

livestock animals kept for use or profit, such as farm animals

mainstream popular

missionary person sent overseas to spread their religion

morals how people decide what is good and what is bad behavior

nomadic people who move from place to place to find food and water for themselves and their livestock

nutrient source of good health for the body

offering gift given during a religious ceremony

orphan child whose parents are both dead

plateau large, flat area of highland

proverb short statement of truth

ritual part of a religious ceremony that follows a set pattern

rural related to life in the country

shrine special place to worship

slave person who is forced to work for another for no pay

textile cloth or fabric

trade buy and sell goods

trance dreamlike state

urban related to town or city life

urbanization process by which towns and cities grow and develop

warrior person engaged in a battle or fighting for a particular cause

Find Out More

Books

Barber, Nicola. *World Cultures: Living in the African Savannah*. Chicago, Ill.: Raintree, 2008.

Bowden, Rob. *Africa South of the Saraha*. Chicago, Ill.: Heinemann Library, 2008.

Friedman, Mel. *Africa*. New York, N.Y.: Children's Press, 2009.

Gritzner, Jeffrey A. *North Africa and the Middle East*. New York, N.Y.: Chelsea House, 2006.

Solway, Andrew. *Africa*. Chicago, Ill.: Heinemann Library, 2008.

Websites

BBC World Service
www.bbc.co.uk/worldservice/africa/features/storyofafrica
This site explains the history of Africa and its people.

PBS Africa for Kids
http://pbskids.org/africa/
Learn about kids in Africa from kids in Africa and learn some activities related to African culture.

Soweto Gospel Choir
www.sowetogospelchoir.com
The Soweto **Gospel** Choir was formed to celebrate African gospel music, using talented singers from the churches in and around Soweto. You can learn the choir's song lyrics on this website, and find out where they are performing.

Places to visit

Many museums have good collections of African art and **culture**. Here are some of the more famous ones:

Museum for African Art
36-01 43rd Avenue at 36th Street
Long Island City, NY 11101
Tel: (718) 784-7700
www.africanart.org

National Museum of African Art
Smithsonian Institution
P.O. Box 37012 MRC 708
Washington, DC 20013-7012
Tel: (202) 633-4600
http://africa.si.edu

The Museum of African Culture
13 Brown Street
Portland, ME 04101
Tel: (207) 871-7188
www.africantribalartmuseum.org

Index